NORTH & EAST
Daybooks

Andrew Mossin

SPUYTEN DUYVIL
NEW YORK CITY

North & East: Daybooks
Copyright © 2021 Andrew Mossin
ISBN 978-1-956005-37-0
All rights reserved. Neither this book, nor any part thereof, may be reproduced by any means without the written permission of the author.
Cover photo: *Gravity* by Ken Taylor ©2021

Library of Congress Cataloging-in-Publication Data

Names: Mossin, Andrew, author.
Title: North & East : daybooks / Andrew Mossin.
Description: New York City : Spuyten Duyvil, [2021] |
Identifiers: LCCN 2021048626 | ISBN 9781956005370 (paperback)
Subjects: LCGFT: Poetry.
Classification: LCC PS3563.O8858 N67 2021 | DDC 811/.54--dc23
LC record available at https://lccn.loc.gov/2021048626

To Joseph Donahue

To perceive……
Is to stand on the edge
……………………..to recognize
contingency
                George Oppen

Preface

> The art of the poem, like the mechanism of the dream or the intent of the tribal myth and *dromena*, is a cathexis: to keep present and immediate a variety of times and places, persons and events. In the melody we make, the possibility of eternal life is hidden, and experience we thought lost returns to us.
>
> Robert Duncan, *The H.D. Book*

I have lived for the last 15 years in a townhouse community that rests at the junction of North and East Streets in Doylesown, Pennsylvania. At various points in my time here, I've stopped at the town of Stockton, New Jersey on the way back to Doylestown from points south, driving back up NJ Route 29 from Philadelphia past Washington's Crossing and through Lambertville on the way to Stockton and the bridge that crosses back over to Pennsylvania. On occasion, I've parked my car in Stockton and walked the Delaware & Raritan canal path that moves alongside the Delaware. In the springtime, leafy ailanthus and ash trees overhang the canal path and wildflowers grow among the felled trees and scattered trash left by tourists. If you continue walking south from Stockton along the river you eventually come into the town of Lambertville, New Jersey. Across the river you can see the condominiums of New Hope as the windows from each building catch the late afternoon sun.

Heading back to Pennsylvania across the bridge in Stockton, you can observe the slow-moving currents of the Delaware passing underneath. After heavy rainstorms, the water level of the river can approach the underside of the bridge as both shorelines disappear from view, the trees at an angle leaning across the river's surface. When you reach the other side, you can see the waters carrying tree limbs and other debris down river.

Book I

Book I

There are few words—
    chromatic stillness
  of the wren
      in late morning

    angular rocking
of the myrtle tree
      scratching gutters.

I would come back
  from these early
scenes, wearing little
    but a shawl   sandals

from another era.

◆

As we read from Canto LI
    to take heart, build from
  an image of God   build the spring
      of paradise in our heart.

◆

Rain fall   wind   color of daylight
    in springtime…

      'dark fur from a hare's ear'

To tease out the particulars as they
      manifest themselves—
  slow-moving waters
          of Chesapeake

  melded with Delaware—
    low lying barge of light
   weathering another storm

      and green waters
     of evening's tidectical
         draw.

◆

   'Our stay in the
   world'—an economy
     of sound that renews

   each instant in thirds.

◆

To translate spirit
  we halved self—

poured biography into a cup

to give it words the world
we said would drink us
into itself, the words
  would become viable again…

◆

In the astringent morning

   light, where materials are, the low

hills of zonal Athens—

'And under the almond trees gods
with them'
Gathered at river's edge.

◆

Where the rain was a seventh
of what water had become, we
couldn't say how long

dreaming was part of our beginning—
each day farther from the road, route
we said we were taking

to become this principle of drift
this reckoning among ghosts, real and unreal
emerging as one body
of water....

◆

A wave of yellow light crossing through

night's door, to begin in pitch & cleanse our
tools in the sharp reds & yellows of night, fold our tent
into the shape of moon squares

lying low by the eastern river
where the bending flowers are
wet on the sloping shore.

◆

      As if
weeping were song

moved through each raised reed
cool as water from triadic Euphrates.

And in Herodotus we read
of the effort to materialize

their protection, building the moat
that encircled their ancient city

Of Babylon.

◆

Yet the dream was
      that & part of what we

couldn't dream up, part
      consequence, part reverie

as if turning inside the
      River Is another river was

lighting the way, source
      of deportation's language

burning where the river
      turned, mouth of salt & bitumen

bitter on the tongue to taste
      red salt water flakes of bitumen.

◆

    All this light
may remain, we say the
          starvation tune

      is apt, the red
skirt, bell of sound, light
         song of the mourning dove

      in evening…We
untravel this distance, this cross
        light, river

      where the hand goes
still, River Is that becomes Was—
         as we turn toward

      snow at the river's mouth
woods covered in jade frost
         our small boat floats away.

◆

The politics of light
    is the parallelism
  of experience—

To inhabit the same
    space, heartfelt
  spirit, build the

habitual record out
    of mental time
  scarcely visible

to the naked eye, lived
        apart from sanction
    or recollect

this revenue of water & sky.

    ◆

        Not out but
toward—

Your decade weathered
        or overly read
    for what it couldn't

reveal: 'In the eyes dream'
        Rilke writes of his
    father as a young man

revealing the long space
        between yearning
    and fatalism—

inert as a wheel of red
        clay, the forehead
    tilted back, shaved

neck, cool at the water's edge.

    ◆

        We are waiting
        you said
            for disappearance.

Earthly colors that fade
       where water is ageless
   our pathways through
           peaches and plums

recognizable Calamus isle.

◆

        And light 'moves on the north
sky line' and 'across the full ornamental
        braids' of his uniform

      My father's hands, at ease, resting
level with his jacket's hem
       forest green on blue.

◆

And all of it
September or the earth
    is resting between

seasons, sumac & oak
inside a ring of light
      unimpeachable

from our window every
branch is resting between
     fronds of red

uneven color. The history
of this perception—
 radicalism's shadow—

cut from wind sheer, the rain
isn't yet a presence

◆

 In the *Pekaj*
we bend among its naming for days
 a flower wind shell

 inside circle, pin broken
from its cloth, loose on the ground
 red as amber shell

 scattered at the river's edge.

◆

'Mouth is a sign' we read
 for the first time our hands
 filled with flowers from the

 cracked river, inside our body...

◆

Skin is emplaced here as

 Water lily serpent wind quetzal serpent

are pillaged, in the turning mouth
      of river light, cloth through the
  hands, writing on the sides of

    our human body....2 days can bring 12...

Overcast, in the breaking dawn
      to reveal the power of hands

writing their way back to

        Deer   Pride   Artisan

◆

    What combines
    appetites—

      surrounding our

    physical space   paratactic light

    folds   writing on the flesh

    of animal skin   our frightened

    soul accompanied   by mouth

    rasp sand wax   underneath a pillar

    'the sound of the word'   inverted

    4 more days bring 12

◆

      Grey scale of the wind
that rises behind us....

                    Seventh morning song rising....

◆

      If this is
      rope, the river

      can't be
      far from

      emergence.

We put our heads together.

We lay these things side
by side...in the magic waters

of Chesapeake & Delaware
we chart the way

'circling in the eddying air.'

◆

A black lake the seventh
to be seen, Saturn in the

    red evening sky, tilts
our heads upward…

◆

        We remember we are
in company….the words are not
            our own…

A score of 6 days brings 8.

        Writing on the walls
in this month of no destruction
           we are keeping summer

        with us, pale where the mouth
is discretionary, to reveal the white latex
           of its flower

        that gives off this scent, incarnadine
black in the red car with jewels
           this bright arc of
                    winter light.

◆

        Scar wood, pale
soft fig, cool cypress
           under red moon

        A name threaded
from many—
           black lake

        Seventh moon.

♦

    And death and spirit

        are split down the middle....

As birds hover in the myrtle tree.

           Outside our window a doorway
           cut from pine needles...

♦

    Light at the river's edge.
    Delivered to its basin
         a falcon's wing

broken from a column of reeds
             enters heaven.

                        SEPTEMBER 28, 2019

Book II

Book II

To rename the world
is to keep time with its objects—

    in the unseen lapses
  where one is going
        between not

    among, this allowance
decades ago, some
        beginning less

    raised than real, bordering
  how many from that first
        encounter to

  this...

◆

    We were raised to under-
  stand so many variances
    words could offer routes

  into another landscape, your
    house or mine, the real
weather is uncanny, to plant ourselves

  between decades, the way we are
    permitted so few, to come
back in springtime—

    this action taken among
  trees—white ash & linden—smeared
      with crayon

                'the Pleiades almost
nameless….the moon tilted
                    and halfgone.'

        ◆

                Over time everything
        happens over time—

            Water through one's
        hands, night is a lesson in
                    reading signs

            after the fact, to draw water
                from a well, seen what it
                    can become

    wheel of water in the white
                still well, to draw light from
        a screen, built across low land

                the object is to see the
        light fill the well, to undo the body's
                    drift, tossed back

            an age is one part of another's
                    husband, common as any.

        ◆

                So it was lush land
        beyond words, saved from inside
                    a tunnel, mesh

      & grey plastic, found
underneath, like a perimeter that
         gave itself away

     drawn across the grass
branch, pale as light that follows
       a man down

   way past his time.

◆

The year moves like
a circle, moving east
    on a train, red sun

come 'round, come back.

◆

     Red so you can
see it, raised scar
       hands are

   raised to offer
light from skin, veiled
      marks on

   hands' surface, right-
side-up, loosened
      scales gone

grey as locust bells.

◆

    'The wind' writes Thoreau
'comes from the N.W. & is bracing
        & encouraging—& we can

    now sail up the stream. Flocks
of bobolinks go tinkling along
        about the low willows

    & a kingbird hovers almost
stationary above the water'
        [Friday August 19th '53]

◆

    I came here
to resist rest, to write
        water back

    yellow on river's
frontis, nameless journey
        we can walk

    age over, near the
beginning, thirsty for
        hard cider

    the road rises to catch
you—

        'a long progress all the stages of a life'

  if you visit often
words can minister the
    descent of miracles.

◆

   Night evacuates
the last, refuge is a skipping
    stone

   sent back across
where August ends, the tones
    obliterate other

  sounds, come less often—
Hawk circling above
    wind is its calendar

  Wing's ash
ascending with each
    flight

  of the kingbird, slow
    in the white morning
   river light

  composed & steady.

          OCTOBER 18, 2019

Book III

Book II

       What is memorable
from a day
              returns as light.

Usual walk this morning up to Doylestown cemetery, down and across past Our Lady of Mount Carmel Catholic church. Cool morning, mid-50's. Maples in full leaf now, sycamore and elms to follow. A world of color....

       Stopping on way back
to see an open grave waiting
              to be filled....

       Cheap utility carpeting
leading up to the
              bier, steel pipes

       across which they'd
laid green belts
              to lower the coffin

       into the hole...
Stopped to look into
              white painted

       wood, oblong
to fit the coffin
              rested inside its

       site. Strange to
see its surface, as if
              one had already

left…but one was
returning.

       Claud "Bud" Young
       1923—

Death date not
       yet engraved.

◆

Our mother's family name   Alford

History of it as an object
lesson   emplaced

over another's…as Dickinson
puts it   'You see I cannot see – your lifetime –

I must guess'

The ancient arms of Alford has the blazon
of a red field, charged with a silver cross
moline. The first recorded spelling of the
family name is shown to be that of Robert
de Aldeforde, which was dated 1184, in the
Annales Cestrienses Rolls of Lancashire and
Cheshire, during the reign of King Henry 11,
known as 'the church builder', 1154-1189.

♦

'The "I" is my unexamined label for the introverted
function of myself that thinks such thoughts. That is
to say, I think it's me. Still do.' (Roy Fisher, in conver-
sation with John Kerrigan)

'What is happening?   I do not know.
Out there where we can see nothing.'

Today inside the box of words   whose
effort did I make out
                visible invisible being—

my eyes on the surface   land absorbing light.

♦

Just as one moves
across the page   the way light
is handle and bowsprit
at the same time   another is
holding a page of letters   the language

comes close to rhapsody   or nearer
to its center   when a slow crease
emerges between   here & there

♦

'my agenda consists in not having one'

◆

Hard to see through
it—

sometimes I'm walking   hands in pockets
the air   sometimes   I'm walking
hands in pockets

See the world
anew…

◆

At a crossroads   the light
is crossed over   my hands falling   replenished

in a 'map of morning and winter light.'
Dear winter, it's 5:15 AM. Spring is 16
days away   I hear roses in the garden
bed   dry leaves   waiting to bloom.

◆

How did a name   go by? so quickly to realize   days
are common now   to deny reality   when the words
sink in   a woman's voice outside   another's in   so many
hours in a day   you can't control the volume…

'But come back
sit….it's the un-
steadiness
that repeats
itself…'

◆

The rest of the poem I'm reciting by heart—

>   *Meet me by the sweetbriar,*
>   *By the mole-hill swelling there;*
>   *When the west glows like a fire*
>   *God's crimson bed is there.*
>   *Meet me in the green glen.*

Which is to say
it was enough
to read

low and lower
on the hill
where he

was put.

MAY 13, 2020

BOOK IV

Recognition   as things
        pass on—

In this glimpse   of where we
could be   against a wall of shadows

inside the house   you are saying so
the work is here   outlasting us

again & again   the propositional
truth   'you can stand up inside it'

awhile ago   when you first read
of cinders   you knelt perhaps

on uneven ground   At 63 to see
my father moving across   his hands

open   holding berries, string, a pack
of cigarettes

These days of reliquary   justice.

◆

The birth-
mark   headstone

One is above
& below

equidistant from
heaven.

♦

The citrus tree in memory
is a citrus tree in

memory. Going inside
to reveal its nominative care

Who is ready to learn?
What isn't here?

♦

The daily forecast...sitting awhile
to learn of what's to come....hearing

my wife's voice from upstairs....low
to the ceiling....vocation separated

by floor. 'We live in nomadic
unfulfillment'

or we perpetuate exile, here
& again, the slow congress

of light...migratory instinct
outlasting the event   Our long

will to survive   every change

'The fact is we are hopelessly
caught in phenomena'

A round of lightning followed
by blue skies   as if every hour

moved separate from every other.

◆

I am less able to return
the favor.

As you would say, 'the work is enough
to get you by'

so much traction across how
many years….here & there recognition

of the real.

◆

      'It's called Wall Street
because the Dutch built a
defensive wall out of wood.
The forest was hickory,
chestnut, oak, sycamore…
From there north around
where Nassau Street reaches
Fulton Street, there were
tulip trees, 100 or 150 feet
high.' (*NY Times* 5/14/20)

◆

And somewhere was the Collect
Pond—

    'sitting within this amphitheater
of hills protected from the winter winds.
The water was fresh, very deep—maybe
80 feet deep—fed by springs.'

Irrecoverable either way   here as
then   later as here

Whitman saw it June 1878—

    'Out today on the waters for a sail in the wide
bay, southeast of Staten Island—a rough tossing ride,
and a free sight—the long stretch of Sandy Hook, the
highlands of Navesink, and the many vessels outward
and inward bound...'

        among 'careening things of grace and wonder, white
            and shaded swift-darting fish birds'

◆

'waves
are not the same as deep water'

◆

    At midpoint the
month goes   inside color wheels
        hand over hand

You could say there's
decisiveness   in wind

        a respite when it fails   stops
turning   over and under
           the ridged underside

of a single hand.

◆

'There are so many
who want to go back'

as if to say   my father's name
Ryszard   a pull in the chest

when he is back   on the
surface of things

'The air works on all men...'

Unhoused by loss
not so much memory but

re-collection, as if to spread
oneself on grass at dawn

& await visitation.

◆

I have no good place left (you didn't say this)
but this one   word after word

      without heroism   leaf scrapes

Human interior?   A shy care is
working out its method   Slow to realize
what it meant   to say   'Ah, you saw it

           alright.'

◆

What do these days want
of us   roaming across the landscape

of another's language   I'm hearing
inside the room   her sharper separate

tongue   'this is my American labyrinth'

as if to remember   one is always
worldless   at the edge

    so back cycle to find
a house still standing
        in a clearing of balsa

narrow bands of yellow where
our life stood.

MAY 14, 2020

Book V

I rode across the landscape   a child
of two   of no one   I
am not one   person

in whose room may I
exist?

Everything could become
          another thing, in time the
     emptying out is
               part of what's left—

'scrape away, scrape away' as Williams put it

To find the world again
you need light   a shovel
earth to dig into.

◆

               And my mother was & wasn't
saying a thing   so often she'd sit
in the garden   her back to
the house

          glass of gin   cigarette in hand

The picture doesn't change   yearly
I could say   the objects are the same
as if by arrangement

               one eye looking down

               one eye looking over

◆

Imagine yourself as two she'd say now
imagine one the art of being two
being one imagine the world as if
you did belong

        Roses laid end to end
      make a pattern on the ground
                  partnership & keys

to an abandoned house.

◆

'A temple built to the glory of
illusion

under the protection of banished
spirits'

      (notebook entry 1990)

Whose name he was recognizing   old
pages of a notebook   he's keeping
this record
          ash-silver lines looped across a wom-
an's
            mouth...

◆

'Let's not go in. It frightens me, this permission
to return by the minute, across exploded bridges.

I push no further, sweet master,
Courageous memory, sad songskeleton.'

   —not going in—

   Is that the same as
returning? or does the light
          shift our purpose—

   hidden from view
in the bushes, formless
          somehow—

   that child you
said you couldn't let back
          inside, here

he is, back again.

◆

Ohio night I was coming
back—
      to sit in the wooded
    circle of darkness—

Not waiting for any
thing, no one's place
      above or below—

only repeating back 'the glory of the stars and the
completely
      rounded moon, silver and luminous-tawny—
      now and then masses of vapory illuminated
      scud—and silently by my side, my dear friend.'

◆

Habitual as night is
shared—memory of
my partner's face
   averted from my
      eyes—

Taken for who we are
   invented from pure
 denial

as we are taken
for another.

◆

'How easy to slip
into the old mode—'

   awake inside the pond
 light, delivered, broken
     across my hand

  a blend of light
and dark, strains seeing, at all
     points west as the road

comes forward to meet us.

            MAY 15, 2019

Book VI

> All who have gone before me,
> Vessels of the billion-year-long
> River that flows now in your veins.
>
> Kenneth Rexroth, 'The Lights in the Sky Are Stars'

What is that thing farthest
from us—

    To remember history
of these itinerant selves
          waking   abandoning
      ash   fabric   washed in the sun

Time slips across
landscape...

Old colors return   blue teal yellow
      & sea flowers above
          the Chesapeake shore.

♦

The refusal of one
or another
person.

Imperfect
skin makes
an impression

tonal singularities
of regard...

◆

Not waking but doing the work
of waking—
  to recall its papery elemental
 scar whitening out dawn light as an episode
    of becoming—

'Turn, toward me, your face.
Is the universe really this small?'

◆

Nothing can build from water
a shelf resists canyon light
we remember it was
the track down
caused difficulty—

shrub rock & cactus

Dusk at the canyon's
floor. Setting up our tent
low to the site's edge...

◆

  To wake in the absoluteness of nothing.

  Empirical sleight of hand. Run
  our hands through coyote willow arrowweed seep willow
    western honey mesquite, & catclaw acacia

      Attending to what was once
  a path of knowledge—
              celebrated in its absence.

◆

Rejecting earlier
forms of the poem   to say
there is this intent

to re-envision
materials   inside
a slow-burning

fire….

◆

In the hour
of our death   I would have it said   ' I want to separate

you from You'

◆

     'I come here to listen, to nestle in the curve of the roots
in a soft hollow of pine needles, to lean my bones against the
column of white pine, to turn off the voice in my head until I
can hear the voices outside it: the shhh of wind in needles,
water trickling over rock, nuthatch tapping, chipmunks digging,
beechnut falling, mosquito in my ear, and something more—
something that is not me, for which we have no language.'
                        Robin Wall Kimmerer, *Braiding Sweetgrass*

◆

A border crossing—

no magic but the empathy
of thought's call   inquiry

stripped of tone   'the place where crying begins'

The arrangement of a body   in place with its owner
godless at the perimeter   of a wall   dividing
one from another

◆

That one can admit
so little
        of consequence

taken apart by the years
we save scraps   paper over
a design   left unfinished

Our mother's lot   to carry
each motif backward   irises planted
late in the year
                came back at summer's end

Her days 'a slit of light
        at no bird dawn'

◆

I am caring   for the little
pieces   spaced a day

apart   days apart   one
brings a terracotta pot

outside the geraniums inside
soil   water   the pot placed

on the ledge facing east…

Simple.

◆

I don't know any
other way   but to follow

these objects   this curious object
skein of plain twine

once seen at a yard
sale   picked up

for a few cents   recall
its pliant weight

its circumference
in the hand.

♦

As Niedecker
understood   to lessen

the weight   you have to
isolate   yourself from others

bend where water
moves   across the marsh bed

like a map of something
seen once   in pictures

from another world.

      'Something in the water
      like a flower
      will devour

      water

      flower'

♦

'Each of us reaches for the place,
reaches the place that they can.'

◆

All things being
equal   A decade

isn't much.

   One day   you will
  return   with a book
      in hand—

not this one perhaps another
   will be a book you
  want to sit down

     & read.

◆

Events can't be traced
   when the pages yield
  silences in place of
     narrative   you

not yet married   living on your
  own   what would you need
     to see

  in the book of images

where these men & women appear
    disappear   all at once?

There's habit   and the refinement
        of a lifetime of habit.

◆

What can invention
prevent   age breaks

across the margins
of thought   saying some

necessary things   habit
to write down

a life   here & there
some truths   shared

in the shadows
of Mt. Tamalpais

as if to recall its formation
noontime's   threaded layers of light

where Rexroth is writing
'Orion again walks into the sea…'

                                        MAY 16, 2019

Book VII

Starting With Lines By Paul Blackburn

'The stone steps down to town washed
                              in her light, the
ribbon of road curving out far below, white
                    white'

That is awkward to re-produce
language   at this hour   what will
remain   instead of 'I'
                someone is waking

inside a room—

          Majorcan sun

          my mother at day's end or thereabouts
          her head cradled in my
                              arms...

Has it been habit to
remain here?   where she & he have
gone   as I said to M. the night
is heavy with them

          what will leave us be?

          and when?

◆

Hidden from view   one is no more son
than father   no more wife than mother

Can we consume these things   re-read them
at the steps of the ancient church   we visited in Rome
spending the entire afternoon
                    in not-prayer   in not-meeting

Lifting the pages of a hymnal   we couldn't read...

◆

Robin song

I can carry so little of that tune

remembering his eyes   following

hips of a stranger   It's simplicity

that eludes   just to remain present

'That means you're never here.'

Or here only insofar as *there* is *here*

written over.

◆

Moving out into the day   light
from the east   low winds   bamboo

chimes   scattered leaves of apple
blossom   in full bloom...

It's the cadence   of time passing   your
voice is after all   one among many others

I have heard   in passing   no one
tone can remain   our memoried body

lifts itself back   moves out into the
new old day   the light from the east

low wind that rises   bamboo chimes
scattered apple blossoms

these arrangements of form

◆

Blackburn   said it was 'lights   the
lights   the lonely   lovely
fucking   lights'

As I tune in   to what the years
bring   turned to what the life treats

Our *Tao* that might emerge   forward
of some things   Your hair   recollected

not seen   Is that the way of it?
Your hair   recollected

not seen?

♦

When Virgil is never far from
the writing table   scraps I'm collecting

over the years   reading *Georgics*
to seal some gap   a telling

that might remain   told
over again   where earth is

in a garden   plot barely 6 by
10 feet   planted with rose

jonquil   hosta   hydrangea
out of sequence   color

emerges randomly

    If she walked here   what would
    she say?   walking back across the
    sloping yard   to stand   inside
    a circle of greens & reds   paler yet

♦

    When we're waiting
for the day to come   here & there
        the yellowing

   light—

        so much moves so
effortlessly, you can't watch the light long

or see its breakage at the

opposite side of a field

in which you are standing   provisionally

brought to your senses

◆

Only 'in hill
territory…for soil
of scant gravel
chips'

bend down to
gather cinnamon
rosemary, tufa
and chalk

wear your linen
blouse
& simple

shoes to walk outside…

◆

The flowers of May then June when you went away….
I gathered them into a bouquet with twine.

◆

    So I'm sure days   are working time
    to settle at the table   these hours of a day
    inside or
                     out where my father is
        sitting in his chair
                     porch-bound in
              Levittown, PA…

    I am revisiting the days   working here is
    respite   the garden he kept   like my own

    a visible small patch of ground

    few flowers to see   weeds in place of
    them   I take some time to gather

                in place of flowers these few stems

    If he is listening   he is out of
    earshot

            a game played between elders….

◆

As we read in Saramago—

'the varnishes and the crucifixes on the lid will have to be
left for the second phase, when the pressure
of funerals starts to diminish…'

Where the bodies are put   we read of the 200
bodies   come through the back
doors of the Farenga Brothers Funeral Home
in the Bronx…

      The bodies come from nursing homes   apartments
houses   and from refrigerated trailers…

           And to find one body among the dead
you had to roll one body off another again and again
              to find one   at the bottom of the pile.

◆

'There has to be some dignity
in this, otherwise I might as well
be a garbage man.'

Not to understand   but say it's happening

against this backdrop of ordinary life   the realism

stacked against the possibility of narrative   so you can't begin

one story and end another   here in the back of a refrigerated

trailer in Manhattan   in April

          'You must have good nerves'   my father might
          have said   knowing what it meant

            to live there.

                        MAY 17, 2020

Book VIII

And everything is thickness
in mind   you can say the days are
movement enough   to count down
the way as children we
separated our fingers   2 4 6
to make 10

So much returns   doesn't it? or are we
fatally out-of-touch?

        'The darkness wins'

you wrote   and I sat for hours inside
the sanctuary of what followed

                                'We live
in the near-winter dark, live near each
other in the darkness...'

Like the gulf between   your house & mine
the enablement of our days   is to resume
what was taken   scent of that room   July
we lived alone   for a period of days
separated from anyone   else   & carried
only some paperbacks   a pocket knife   glasses
to read thru the night.

   ◆

Nostalgia for the dead?   Their loss
you could say   to come out of the daylight
                        Easter Sunday   a paradox

of shadows along Calvert Street

as downtown   became another world
for us to visit

         My father lay down   & mother beside his
         body   to enumerate their days
         here again   suddenly   we are leaving the
         avenue   with so little ability to hear   their cries

     O light!   simple as your eyes
     and direct   as my mother's pale skin
     against my own   darker

◆

Against our will   charmed
you said   light is charming when it
     falls   full force   across our body

awake for awhile   sees out
of one eye
     as if we could trespass   here
         nude in the dawn light

◆

The cities we knew

To hear the crisis each
     proposes—
   as if living in limbo
       with each set

Of days....

♦

A geography that can't be
retraced   here among the dying

The spaces open out   up   retrieve
the bodily   walking down the park-lit
piece again in Philadelphia 1992

locust trees in bloom   summoning
their term

Everyone gone inside   doorways
bathed in autumn light

Is it ceremonial justice   affords us
this quiet   burial time?

♦

'You can't have it both ways' my
mother said   to have it
         at all   limits are
   3 x 10 x 12   when you count
that far   you can see

                roof light   church spire of St. Alban's
          near evening   & the low chiming
                           bells of evening Mass.

♦

'Let me be alone here.'

        The energy it takes

69

to say 'let me be'
                'alone here'

There is a structure
for all things
        we say /
                don't say.

I want to believe
words will make a difference.

Alone. *Here.*

◆

Each note is a turn
toward the other side
of the river…

If any world comes back   ours
is this one   of meeting
                      separate & alone

◆

As the days proceed   'road
after road   without retreat.

Access only to those
you have before you….'

Not claim but the spare trace
passed back to   our dead.

MAY 18, 2020

Book IX

Daylight   plane flying low
over head   a stream of light
       clear to the treeline's edge

I have these things   for you
writing them into the screen

Day work   how can it be
                otherwise?

◆

In some picture
of the self   crayoned
into
      leaves   the book

left open   on the ground

'Here,' you said, 'find the green
space'

      Not so much order
   but the choice of materials
         loose charcoal grain
      inside the margins

        in loose hand, 'just this'

◆

So we came to be
reading Propertius   because Taggart
said it was necessary   to live

inside another's language   He said to
come back
          inside song   you must wreathe

the words back through your
                palms   let them brush

   surfaces of night song   *saintless*

let the storage place   come to fulfill you

'in the soft shade of Helicon, where flows
the fountain of Bellerophon's horse'

To listen intently   where the dream
is insistent & private
          & each stone rests   near water.

◆

Inside a field   meteor light
a dance   my heart came

to its stillpoint….

◆

And this is public   light we are saving
outside of view   righted on ground
left by others—

I am caring for my dead
to carry them across with me

shepherded by their weight.

◆

Loose wisdom   Olson would have
said   not much use here
                'where you taking that?'

Box of leaves   saturated by
well water
        left underneath a rock ledge.

◆

        Crows on the iron
feeder post   rock side to
                side—

    slid back their   beaks raised

        in cracked   unison

        staring into the light.

◆

I have little
memory   the problem
is to remember
        how long here

and the way back....

Our children come to us
or say they will
re-visit

hourly by the bell.

◆

Erasing the separation   between here
& then   weighted options
           they foreclose identity

I want to live inside   their passage

loose   itinerant   birdlike

           streaming from the edges
       of a pastoral scene
               I can't resume
           but believe will come.

◆

And always we said   it was 'beginning's
beginning'   we'd schemed to
           revisit   coming abreast of
'beginning's ghost'

           There's a tale we're sketching
outside where the marbles got
               played   late sun was
a relayer   of signs
all come home.

◆

My color is not
yours   or any other

but a surface of
light   pooled from below

the water refracts
surface & light

to begin there...

◆

And sweet violet
exists   if it exists

exerts pressure
on our reading—

encountered first
in Latin   *inriguumque bibant violaria fontem*

'And let clumps of violet
drink the welling spring...'

Earth light cracked
in two   inside each line

the ribbed nature of one.

MAY 19, 2020

Book X

         'The Sun will give Signs
both when rising and setting
into the waves   the surest
signs shall ensue from the sun'

In the rhythm of its making
I can't say if I hear
           language at all—

but in private   talking
out loud   the sentences
                as we begin to walk

across a field   in late May
the myrtle still bare
                of blooms

◆

'There is a peculiar softness and luminousness
in the air this morning—perhaps the light
being diffused by vapor   It is such a warm
moist or softened sun-lit air as we are wont
to hear the first bluebird's warble in.'

 Settling in—to the movements
across the decades—light is
surplus—additive—we
break up the line
        to lay down light

seeing the way ahead   these rooms
you might say   starved of light

                in this condensation
            light & sound
                        from inside a field

memorized—

These angles of color   rose & bronze
set back from the surface
                        sea blue in the distance

◆

But to keep
pace   let the poem
become   from what

isn't yet—

The shaping of a lifetime

slivers   sent into the air

slow moving field
rain   showers   nearly
done
        across the treeline

                yellow bands   residual
                color

◆

Rain from one sky
late color from another

        mesmerized by what
    isn't in place—

Slow passage through
a day   another one situated
inside the first

       It's hard to remember   you said
       'I haven't a clue how long'   the lifeline
       was never this   but protracted
       in some sighting of the real   we
       saved how many pieces   to lay
       them down before you   asking
       at each turn   'Worthy?'

There is from before
the learned space   you come
out of it   hard on the days
       weighted by lack—

Each reunion   a foreshadowing....

◆

As one can say   we are 'not here to decorate our age'

An ethics
of composition   guiding language

across the days…

Of one life
what can be said?   there is this
partnership   between saying & doing

as if we came into the room   without
impression   & drew the letters

on pages   palimpsests
of writing.

◆

And beauty?

Solitary   is another opening
out to what follows

'The individual man' Duncan says
'having his nature and truth
            outlined
in relation to groups
appropriate to his household

   his own
   ideogram

   a tuning   in'

◆

Whose nature is   public
to any   and private in its
            temperaments—

'the eye staring back from the other side
waiting'   as surely there is

memory for each death
in life.

◆

      Stillness is this benefit
underneath one's skin
          to house the body—

     bone work that leaves us separate

     bending down   starlight
          not heavens   inside earth.

◆

(memory site)

     At the iron gate to her house   an elderly woman
moving into the street   falling against a spike
        her head   blossoming red

     Fatigued to remember it   so many years ago

     a street lined with locust trees   Shepherdstown, W Va

     Her body as it fell to the ground
     unaccompanied   red jets across
                       June pavement

◆

Thought
doesn't enter into it....

'Loosen the line, let it move
thru you.'

    My mother's hands
    distanced from my own—

  at evening to separate
  again—to walk through
      a line of color—bare trees

  in late May   and

        '—a dark flame,
a wind, a flood, counter to all staleness.'

MAY 22, 2020

Book XI

Book XI

> 'I is the substance must change—
> that is, our sense of it.
> Robin Blaser

The language returns us   day
after day   in these days of
return
          steady rains   from morning
until now   given to write here
these lines

patiently turning...

◆

It is in crosscurrents   as I might
have once rested   in a boat
          headed across the Potomac—

East of my home
west of where I tended
          nothing so simple as bread

or braided rope—

But the prospect of voyaging
out   loose wind   schooled in that
red light
          at dawn.   To come down

without fear   these mornings you are
resting   at one side   of my torso

so much ahead   you say   rites
of passage   these resting places
            clear under the April sky.

   ◆

Everything is in movement
or nothing is—

            'the gulls flying white and black / simply   '

sky cleared   we are returning without
                        a care....

   ◆

'in the trees

      the strength of cross

            winds

                  and then sunlight'

by which Eigner meant

the trees are on
earth   moving without
us....

         ◆

So that any man or woman
I can see   say their names in a cross

wind   sitting cross-eyed   to name

them again   vertical in a slow
coming rainfall   they have their
       places next to me   come back
    to tell me their tales   weighted
          unhappy   distorted

I am gifted by their presences…

◆

And the moon   when we rise
in the middle of the night
       seen from one open window—

partway   a ledge left open
in the distance
         Your hand   you rested near
         mine   'stay'   lifted to return
    where light was forthcoming

◆

The materials   we are saving
so many things   'give things away' you said
meaning   'your things are of no use there'

East of us….the low route
up through town…calm streets
pandemic days…

How to create order from objects
spaced across a field in spring—

Our doors partly open.

◆

      I go back up   the hill   past the Pentecostal
                          church   cemetery stones
from the 1700's

      Black curtains on the windows   closed since
March

The materials   we are saving
so many things
              for another day.

◆

Pitch black   in the sun
light   the days are pitch
black   to square off with our
history   a passing calm

not new to us   this breaking
down of things   violence

never far-off   as language
breaks down   knotted up

piled-up rope left behind.

◆

As if writing were this séance
with our dead   to deploy their
voices
          proscriptive   inverted

Say I came to them in a dream   passing stranger

What would you say
from down there?

MAY 23, 2020

Book XII

Book XII

So that something materializes   is
in this way part of the real   We leave
the door   open   partway

       to catch a breeze   voices from the yard
     become part of the music   inherent   extrinsic

we catch ourselves   half asleep   waiting for them
to begin again….

       as the poet's voice   is part of the realm
          of understanding   entered into   just
       this way   a reality of inside & out
              reacquainting the body
with light.

   ◆

And what comes must be
sufficient
    unto itself—

as in Thoreau we read of 'skaters and
water-bugs [that] finally disappear
in the latter part of October, when the
severe frosts have come'

pond & light   the structure of
a world   for itself only
    this semblance of language

we re-deposit here   years from Ohio
valley autumn   we sat near another body
    of water   low in the wooded part

        & waited for the dark

    to come   draw itself around us

    ground and sky   that inflect one
    another   propose another intensity

        the smallest way forward   on one's hands
                          & knees....

    and the water   'streaked by flakes of light'

◆

There is that world
then this   to gather the days
inside one   then another

region of mind   *What have you got to lose?*

Time gives back   our decades
with salt on them
        earning our keep   'given to write poems'

Creeley said   or poems are given us to write

Either way   a world
small here   enlarged by whatever

we can carry.

◆

Separate readings of self   to assure

no one is watching
                    this rubric of self-isolation

To keep constant the vigil

of language

                the instruct of days

◆

As yesterday   we drove to the Rosary
Garden at Czestochowa   so few
before us   walking past

The Annunciation   in late afternoon

        'What can it mean?' I asked

arrangement of succulents   before each
stone tableau

                'No way to know,' my daughter offered.

We have little memory   of such places
but keep a map   to show

we traveled this way   took note.

♦

The memorials to the
Polish war dead   row after row
as we'd met them before

a narrative of un-naming   historied
as my father's life   resumes

this distance—

'So it is said
            that instead of wooden crosses they have names
planted in space'

Underneath newly planted
poplars   each stone weighted

by emptiness.

♦

Returning to Thoreau
the light   silver through the net
curtains   dull inside each
        frame   a world

out there   we care that it
remain   somehow possible to reach

from this garden   another's light
we say   'revenant'   when perhaps
        we intend something else—

as I find underlined in my
Harper Classics edition   ca. 1976
this language

      'It is a mirror which no stone
can crack, whose quicksilver will never
wear off, whose gilding Nature continually
repairs...'

                walking off in mid-sentence
          alert to the changing light
                      storms from the east

      we lay the book down   its spine split in two
            the pages spilling out   of order.

◆

A public affection   we make
our wares visible   at daybreak   sky
leaks out   from underneath

a basket of roses   I am laying
these leaves in place   saved from
winter   laid over sweet

newly tilled earth   your voice that makes
a circle on the ground

                edged by maple and pine...

                                MAY 24, 2020

Book XIII

Book XIII

A form of adherence   to the ritual
of writing   putting words in line

proposals of a journey   into these strata

Each bend of light   we lean into each
square   throat sound as we clear

our voice   listening into its
cycle   wind song driving us

farther outside ourselves.

◆

If a kind of stillness
can result   if the body
can move
          out of harm's way—

tell the child it's going   without
not punishment   but intellection

in the closed room   saying it
ourselves over & over   nimbus

clouds through an open window
scattered showers   late

days moving across our vision.

♦

Is it aphoristic to say—

One is always away, another
is coming back.

'And now it seems,' Whitman wrote
'the beautiful uncut hair of graves.'

The strangeness of death   to outlast
memory   reference gone

all but here.

♦

Staying here   you were right
to ignore all else   patience in signs
that result from wonder

        we are arguing for gods' place
when out of time we say
           earth is tired of names

let one give back   species as an act
of denial
       understood as abeyance   before the act.

♦

A modality of recollection   recording
the days in passing, reading back
through   Whitman writing in 1864:

'I used to walk at midday hour or two now
and then for amusement on the crowded
and bustling levee, on the banks of the
river...'

Estranged   along the Mississippi
an eye to surroundings   the politics
of that gesture   open & inviolable

◆

Dark stars at midnight   weighted
contrarieties   built of stony cold matter

our worlds contract   diminish
as words fall away...

'When shall I shake off
   bonds of the common
world—
         ride dark seas
         boundless and free?' (Du Fu)

Real time   elides
us   prefiguration

nighttime glissando   river water

& geese

         circling above earth's surface.

◆

'Things are circling back again,' Long Soldier
writes, 'Sometimes when in a circle, if I wish to
exit, I must leap.'

To imagine   space in which our hearts
are re-aligned   in this politics of envisioning

a movement into and through   these landscapes
common memory   common worlds

among the drought-yellowed grasses.

MAY 26, 2020

Book XIV

Book XIV

> The trees showing sunlight
> Sunlight trees,
> Woods ranging forms
>   Zukofksy, "A" [5]

> 'A still and quiet angel of knowledge
> and of comprehension'
>   Oppen, *The Materials*

Begin day's work   here   locate
the readings that can become
part of this time—

We're bending   ourselves
over   these leaves   screened
items   saying they are

        leading the way—

to redistribute the local   slow
across May skies   wheat colored light
incremental   nears completion

in the early noon hours

◆

I was reading again
in *The Plants of Virgil's Georgics*

of salix   common or white
willow   not seen in these parts

purple osier   *salcio da vimini*

'Like the soft siler and the
plant broom, the poplar and hoary
willow beds with whitening leaves'

To form an image of them   in mind
the way waters cross the landscape

pouring in even waves   of water
currents forming even waves

of grey matter   light inside
each vessel   the human hand

that draws down   to feel its passing.

◆

'In rivers grow willows'

a bird passing   sky loose with
cloud   heavy rains to come

not morning   turning away
from inside its hours

eidetic time   we are spared
loose coinage   to realize

time's weight   in every river
the passage of honey.

◆

'Dragging the piles of willow
branches away, I was removing
storehouses of nutrients they
had sucked from the pond
bottom. The brush pile in
the field grew taller, soon
to be browsed by cottontails
and redistributed far and
wide as rabbit droppings.'
    Kimmerer, *Braiding Sweetgrass*

Invention   of the place

is word for the place   inhabit

the word stream   let their beings

drop into view

◆

       'Heartswork' you said 'depends on clarity of purpose'

to return at evening   the same way

we entered the scene   leaving nothing

disturbed.

◆

Replicating the days   as silent
acumen   border song

    here in the alphabet barn

where we hear 'voices / blown away'

so simple to reproduce   cadence   at arm's
length   another is waiting to resurrect

the body   lower it into the ground

Water   rhythmic dance of molecules
        a forest of pine   maple   elm

◆

    And do you
twist past Hesiod's acumen

from the *Oxford Book*
of Greek Verse   opened to—

> 'When the jar is just begun
> when the jar is nearly done,
>   Drink at ease;
> Halfway down it, drink with care;
> 'Tis poor husbandry to spare
>   Of the lees.'

As one might   leave the book
open   find the right
    position to turn

back   Here & there the intricate
                    piloting—

Our mind's crossing   low to the east
                              habitual light.

◆

If I said   later is enough

waking without a time   lost

hours

            You cross the road at dawn   desert flowers
         banded in a small bouquet
                        I was reading Hesiod from an old
               edition   keeping time to his rhythms
                              Works & Days

            incipient   small lamp placed at the desk's edge

         preparation for evening

Reading of Aeolus winds....crossing
north by southwest.

◆

Willows rich in withes

  et glaucus salices

And pale green willows.

 ◆

Was remembering door
sign post lost to another
era—
   errata scribbled on the backs
 of envelopes
     we are saving scraps of things

 'you may need these one day' our father said

putting them away
inside boxes glassine wrapped
addenda to their lives.

 ◆

   Yesterday moved into the garden

    light maneuvering of plants

   into place the season

     barely begun

   planting tomato and eggplant

   A summoning of our body

to emerge   in the 5 o'clock shadows

        loose governance of time

We are lifted from a woman's arms

    like new material from her hand

winnowed assurances of fate

        & color.

MAY 28, 2020

Book XV

'I appear to reserve a big continent of denial for myself in order to be able to do my work. If I didn't, I couldn't do my work.'
                                        Carroll Dunham

In 'Culture as a Verb'
he writes it out   as paint
still on the surface
            combines textures

of light   'auburn leaves
dangling and falling'
the bottom portion
of canvas
            'ensnared by a red
mass of spirals and curves'

so that one tastes   blood
back of the throat
a totem
                suspended in red.

◆

We're indwelling   bordering
black rainstorm clouds
                a year & a year
after a year

to suspend ourselves
as red matter   a mass inside
that frame   obscure

sadness? stillness of the
wood   we are in-breathing

paratactic leaf by leaf   a shadow
across one daughter's hand.

◆

Dreams are relations   hiding
spots for our unconscious   selves
to appear

        'rain is imminent....storms in the offing'

We are less certain what the words
mean than what they denote   'rain is
imminent....storms...offing'

As if paraphrase and repetition
could displace   the saturated
particulars

◆

There are two daughters   as once there
were two mothers

◆

What unnerves the process
suspends writing   saying one is
liberated by dailiness   the account

must be incomplete   as any
would be   in the wall hanging
you brought back from Istanbul

of the Hagia Sophia   the narrative of
its burning   doesn't appear

twice-burned   rebuilt   the blue
dome all that appears   inside a red

background....

◆

The sound a poem makes   incremental
staggerings   the lines are refuge
false starts   ceremonial bits   unsecured
lateness   this yearning for a
completeness

                only ongoing—

at a late hour   on any given night
we can return   halfway between one self
and another   there is red inside each

torn piece of fabric   a wall hanging
complete unto itself
                a force from inside
that seems to come back to you

as any property   attains its symbolic
value   in the household
a relic   a talisman   charm

situated hereafter.

◆

'There was always another and another
and another'

These knots in the thread
renamed   re-positioned

in endless juxtaposition
We are moving with the sunlight

at late morning   the retractions
and indeterminacy of another's

hand....reaching across the
table   'I remembered them then

I forgot them soon after'

◆

Reaching back   I'm here now
with the work I'm doing   years
are longer   or shorter

             'Keep writing into your 30's
it will be a career'

          someone said to me   in my 30's.

Why not stop? The question

could be addressed   to you
or no one...

◆

'I'm trying to reexamine my early thoughts
about painting and see what it means to me now.
My whole idea about how to make paintings came
from an idea about a diagram of a painting. Painting
as a demonstration model.' (Carroll Dunham)

Because you come back   within the frame
to attest to color   build the network
of red   against red   until the appeal is
negative   into the positive
                      territory—

a form of sweetness   of belated labor
this pilgrimage into color   that is & isn't
materially based.

◆

And if we bend   to the 'practice of stillness'
as Olson called it   forming in place

        or language comes from the
                tidal wash—

reaches us   we are bending into   Chesa-
peake waters
a morning we are standing
            at the edge of a small
                    landing at Sandy Point

◆

There is this refusal   at 4:37 p.m.
this afternoon   as if our body
were that fish   floating
out of itself   in Hesiod's
poem   the fish bronzed
quivering with fear

and the dolphins
giving the impression
            of swimming.

MAY 29, 2020

Book XVI

Book XVI

        Not remembering is a kind of
talk   we make do here   we live inside
               curtains   for days
  it's dusk then light   'Do you know

              where I come from?'

    Lorca asks   where we sit inside
  his hours then our own
                 as if to hide were habit

      here   to run past thresholds of doors

    each occasion begins another   each
             entrance   errant and unknown

When we can live here   among these cold stars
                           & highways   kiss
               the surface   without
                              moving a muscle.

◆

Believe it   the riverbed
mutating under sky.

And wonder   that it's an evening
song   we say it's an event

made from red trees
& clouds   the edge of which

is lyric   a rescued scene
of optic sound   as if we'd

begun the day   pale
like a morning flower

A day lily   bending
soft they say   softer than a bird

crossing red clay at dawn.

◆

      To write it out   we can't   is it farmland
later the emptiness of a field seen from a distance
           'the roots of evening
                      rising'

So unclear   what is here   what's not   these after-
                  day thoughts   abandoned self-study

Of one's place in the world   to say the days
are totalized   grief-worn

plural in their disencumbering

◆

And to reason with oneself
here   in stasis
           waters of the Atlantic

Not remembered but cited   as itinerary
missed turn of one's body

near and far

                    at the edge of land

of it but not in it.

◆

When the dream is open   to interpretation
tired at morning   the embodiment
of these syllables   returning

to an earlier mode

            'east against the source of the sun
in an hour before the sun's going down'

Empeopled here   at land's edge
but not of it.

MAY 29, 2020

Book XVII

Book XVII

That we can assume   so little
of what can we assume   the world
is later   masked   mortal

When we are remembering hunger
as a form of self-giving
         to name the streets we went into   decades ago—

Retracing our footsteps   loose objects
in a line   we haven't time   to say which

is evidence   which relation
to another's map

         Our world, you said
smaller than it once
           was   out of habit or design

Who can say?

◆

'With departing Venus, large to the last, and shining
even to edge of the horizon, the vast dome presents at this
moment, such a spectacle! Mercury was visible just after
sunset—a rare sight. Arcturus is now risen, just north of east.
And now, just rising, Spica, late, low, and slightly veiled.'

The dicta of such movements   into
dawn light   we are less able
          to ascertain   what they may mean.

◆

What's the risk?   Combined with: *How does it appear?*

Is this refuge or hiding space?   Does the poem conceal
or reveal itself? A passage in hand-drawn script....

      There was a street once   I saw it early in memory
building a way up to an alley   a crossing from one side
            to another   and out of view   at
the crest
        of the next hill   the semblance of nextness
        near-to-itiveness....

By dusk the alley was empty again   foreign   as any hour
might be....

◆

Each of us   interspersed
re-endured....

as I return   the way I came through
days at a time sitting
with the Pisan *Cantos*
           the memory of tent flaps   desert
nights

'and a white ox on the road toward Pisa
    as if facing the tower'

whose prayers fell on deaf ears   separate from the route
taken to get here

◆

We are using what we can   here & there in the off-chance
we'll return   a day later   to find something of use.

My hands on the table   the idiom of one
to one   reception poor from radio   we can linger
in the off-seen   small vowels captive sounds

earth is realized as we go   aftermath of the first
light   later another has seized up   beside us

                    his head showered with light
                    from an open window.

◆

'What returned to my thought as I began work this morning was the revelation of the stars. All the stars of the cosmos had come forth from the remotest regions into the visible. At first I was struck by the brilliance of Orion, but as I looked the field was crowded with stars, dense cells of images and then almost animal constellations of the night sky.'

Even as from my window   there are few stars
left   at the ends of sight   we can see

only the formation of rooftops   sealed beneath
a tree line of elms maples poplars

                  the world adventure   asleep in our minds.

◆

      'We have only hope in what is without
remedy. That things are thus and thus—this is
still in the world.'

                    Or we aren't
                    relatable   can't

                    see our skin
                    separate from its

                    skeleton.

◆

The elderly man   we saw today
inside a rim   of white fencing—

I said 'you can walk
back if you know the way'

Smiling   no point
to cross this way again.

◆

Recognizing the effort
                lifelong—

separate from one thing
to another
        each object   held up

to the light.

'All this is obvious, and beyond this—'

JUNE 1, 2020

Book XVIII

Book XVIII

The way the taste of white paste
returns   a foraged instinct

for what happens   somatic
disorder   sense memory is this

dislodgment   ferreted out
scene by scene

      the great weather of mind.

◆

Siting down to write after a storm
has passed   watching it from our
bedroom window   storms clouds

approaching from the west   aqua blue
deepened to purple   near black

before opening—

    the surface is wind   lakes form
from the waters deposited
        our skin is drenched

    inside & out   the miracle
of preservation
        surrendered to light storms.

◆

Everything is a cadence   a report from the
sun   overlying our deaths   the light

makes a corridor   for us to pass through
weighted   sleeve of god's arm

I'm waking near the transport   system
to another range   your voiceless

skin   hieratic nimbus of black
cloth woven from silk   layer upon layer

smoothed by one hand   over another.

◆

I am keeping vigil here   30 days
x 100   the voices may not return
after   a history can exist

separate from its actors   ongoing
sleep   conducts of energy

passing across the earth.

◆

And Thoreau is an advocate
passing with us—

    'From a man in a waking moment—
to men in their waking moments. Wandering
toward the more distant boundaries of
wider pastures—Nothing is so truly bounded
& obedient to law as music—yet nothing so
surely breaks all petty and narrow bounds.'
                     (Feb 5, 1854)

The lake in mind   burning
or half opened to wind
              fires from outlying forests

claiming another 10,000 acres.

◆

  We've surrendered
sundered   place from
habit   to take food
here
        build a shed

in low light

               remake our days—

at risk of saying
little   to others

hearing only   inner counsel

        Angel light

   at the edges

        of our task.

◆

      Where is my *Angelus interpres*?

      Who will come forward   assigned
to this existence   shepherd to Hermes

'Do you no recognize me?'

             'No.'

'I am the shepherd to whom you were handed over.'

      Awakened here   as a stranger
in one   a familiar to no one
            awaiting meeting with our Guide.

◆

The effort to see is a life's
work   voice comes
      iterations of itself

mirrored in objects   cool
morning light   memorabilia

      of the passage

as we read again in Williams

    'It is late
but an odor
    as from our wedding
        has revived for me'

◆

We are these undisciplined

    remainders   of prior life

sent back to reacquaint ourselves   with the mysteries of form.

Shepherded to a room   beyond us—

    the sea   Mediterranean shelf   as one sky

        punctuates the stars   proliferating

points of light   we say the stars are part of the sky

our naked body
        wrapped in leaves.

JUNE 3, 2020

Book XIX

Book XIX

Writing in between   this space   leavened by
2:11 p.m. sunlight   assuring the way
one holds oneself upright
                the materials   aslant   occupied

a place for a time   the woman sitting
beside me   is an image in water

I will transcribe for the rest   of my days

quieter
   the talk
 is endless—

A bird this morning   I watched from
our bedroom   one attends   so quickly
to frame the view…

◆

The logic of the work
is the illogic
of one's mind

separate from each
occasion   the light
is a course

of action   a source
we wrote
based on activity.

♦

      'Last night the thunder
   rolled   wind passed like ten
            thousand crossbows

     together.   It also blew
apart the engulfing cover   in vain
          one sensed that

spirits were gathering.'

♦

To transform   or is it *refine*
by hand?

     The angel at the side   rests   restive

separate talker   we've come to begin again

♦

    As Ed Roberson read his poem
of plywood & fire
         we processed

    changes to come—

this season   of separation   yearning
for the polis   separate inside this
year of separation

   'beginning is what we have in place
  of tragedy'

Cool bodied mouth lit from within
a chamber carrying us ahead

    as if through the distance a body
of water moved through us…

 ◆

What did we say we were invited
to re-read our language terminus of
Greek lettering
    script's hidden purchase

Η Πόλις είναι μάτια

   'Polis is eyes'

All of its meaning encoded
we are writing by the sound of another's voice

Rites where writing is beginning
the absolute crayon
    of betokening—

these lesions in the fabric of our soul.

 ◆

'Breath burned dry
  guts & belly melt
  clothes strained

                  from abundant sweat'

When ritual is performed   these eras
far from his house   a stance we are making
out own   if only to decrease

loneliness   erratum of the lived
imperfect life

            absolute preamble   to the next.

◆

Who sends me   back *there*?

'a terrifying—
a misapprehension—of the presence
and absence of God'

Where the sign   is a Judas knot
of territorial affection

for what betrayal can bring   betrothal's
peace garland   strung
            through the winter night—

Is this yearlong?   a weight
worth pressing?

            To disencumber oneself   late in life

Read the real   for sovereignty   signs

of life on earth.

◆

But I betrayed no one   brought
clothing for a night stay   one is resistant
to such simple realism

      this irreparable station   passing
a library in summer
          our hands reaching out—

Slow combine of skin and paper   the hidden
meaning of early texts.

◆

We are awakened   by first bird song
chickadee and robin
        late for their voices

to arrive—

I am sitting on the bed's edge   water
inside a glass   bottle on the table
next

     lines from Whitman in my head
'and the aromatic cedar'
        'giving something to each'

Names from a compass flower   passed among friends.

◆

What remains?   the property
'compos'd around by a thick
cloud of spirits'

      ornate   creaturely   loose bodied

When can we name their
destiny?   or reach back across
the decades   'twigs of maple and a
bunch of wild orange
and chestnut'

      distributed   handed off again.

◆

The roses   after a storm
are gathered   up

possibly to resume   their color—

Morning was steady   breaking in a line
of nimbus clouds   then sun

expansive across the grass.

◆

Perception   naked to the eye
what can your   lens see?

Difficult to separate   our beginning
point   parish church we grew up
near—

Now the 50 years
one goes less often   to sit

quiet   working our way
to His House.

◆

I want to re-envision
silence   its architectural
simplicity   adrift inside
the nave   a pool of water
by my left hand

I'm drawing
comfort   from beginnings.

◆

Early structures return. Plain
view of song. I have

attachments here. Slow
going they become

visible   circular presences
on a red background.

◆

'Pythagorean idea: the good is always defined
by the union of opposites. When we recommend
the opposite of an evil we remain on the level
of that evil. After we have put it to the test,
we return to the evil. This is what the Gita
calls, "the aberration of opposites."'

And it remains   part of our
work   to see the rites of unacknowledged
opposition   as unities within our work

preserving this uncertainty   the
goal of thought.

◆

The bridge from one thing
to another....or is it

nexus   flight   groundswell
beneath our feet

          so much is left
open to interpretation   clarity

only when breathing stops.

◆

Quotidian realism...remembering the dream
of my father   or were there two

fathers in the dream?

      His face   stern   accepting   careful to look
away from mine
        an outlook I would say later was
    composed of guilt and shame.

Who can say?   His eyes in that
February light   ten days
before his death—

the dream is an excavation   a mine
we enter   unable to find our way
        'in an even more bottomless night.'

JUNE 8, 2020

Book XX

Book XX

> Let's see the very thing and nothing else.
> Wallace Stevens

One moves among
these shadows   turtle doves   robin song

errant flames of color   a garden
      with patches of sun   shade

calmer in the late hours
when I come down   to water

setting light   beginning to form
a circle in the ground   walk-away
as composition.

There's neutrality   to be sure
the ease with which understanding
of the world   reveals itself

locationally—

         this common red

         sky tone   bleached

         rock   riverine

         violets at the edge

◆

And the semantic stretch   recognition
of a face   moves underneath

We're visiting our earliness   to redefine
the lifeline   routes' oblique

terrestrial fold

Night wing   we live inside its
sheathe   a bright nail

carried forward.

◆

The rainfall   this era
this time of year   fails our
accounting

       Winter or summer?

Duration is a principle of accentuation.

We follow the lead of our voice
to undo what it gives   slow-moving
lake water

       a world under construction—

There was this form of sovereignty
we heard of its assignation   motherless

remote as stars   in heavens
light   we sang our hymn

for retention.

◆

Some days   quicksilver
thinking—

others   remote voice

no guidance…

        Working alone   the idea of
separation   neutrality's cycle
            we lay these words

against each other   to find peace.

◆

Eventually to pass over
we are saying in sleep
what the days become
always the days do end
here they come again—

Crisis returns   when the day
is done   we are lying in a garden

out of doors   the elements
of a body   we say there is this

storage   an Arcanum of light
whitened sky   the limit

of our language   to tell what
happened   didn't come back

at all.

◆

So that getting out
could be the first fact

of coming   here   where
no one lives   as sky

attends   ground underneath
wet river flowers

held up to a man's face—

      this jeweled precinct of color

      cool direction of the senses

Moon's rough edges   beamed
back into view   from the ground

below   a scene of mortal
summer.

◆

   And if I am
 this thing
    no one's

     brother or son—

    awake
 when the light
      enters

    this room
revealing itself on
       myrtle

    branches atop
 framed squares
      of light—

    'fertile thing'
  separating itself
     from view.

◆

Everything is part of
the process wind locates the body

far-off track brings it back
into view

    Our clothes covered in mud
    from the trek who will unclean

        our hands   wreck of the woman's
        hands in water   the days

        are vigils for their oncoming   'assignation'
        is a sin   my mother said   her voice

Equal to none.

◆

Light moves across a table   dim
sitting   we are laying ourselves

in wait   to crease the page
again into 4's   leave cessation

like grace   foundering in a drawer.

◆

Areas of reception   memory

is a lake of reading   handled

                            by force—

What is can be recollected   or re-seen?

Vision of the Connecticut River

from Mt. Holyoke   1979 or '80   morning light

traveled to the crest of Mt. Holyoke

catching the river light   & saw

easterly clouds moving across   shadow

forms on a brown map of water.

> As standing at the hill's edge, I caught a passing schooner on the Hudson near Annandale, the light transecting winged tree branches' dip to the river's edge. The duality of scenes, separated by decades, smooth hands on the ground, moss, lichen, the deep hues of milkweed and yarrow…

◆

The man's body
laid to rest.

Leaves and water.

Sun and leaves.

All down the Connecticut River valley…

◆

Words do lead   someway
or other   we combine

what we can   with our
hands   tilted up to

block out the sun

Summer's late   forget-me-nots
in a small bunch

Gathered here   put to
use   all day long.

◆

As if we could step back
inside   windowlight   the ambience
of another's scene

laid bare—

               'It was lighted
in those days by candles especially
made for the show. They were giants fastened
to boards hung on wires about the tent,
a peculiar contrivance. The giant candles
were placed on the bottom boards, and two
rows of smaller candles one above the other
tapering to a point, forming a very pretty
scene and giving plenty of light.'

So that to see Paterson again
is to relive its emplacement   in mind

at the edge of the Passaic Falls.

◆

We are receptors   of others' news
combining reports   from landscapes

we haven't known
                but dreamt of—

this arc of transcendence   at once
residential and habitual

a cadence   memory's long shot
returning from its work

without remorse.

◆

As we are led again
to another view—

      'Clear autumn in the
    Wu Gorges, ten
            thousand ravines lament'

in prayer   at the fault line
of consciousness   recognition

entering this portal   'for security one must
         depend on talents
                beyond the ordinary'

Surviving the centuries   mid-afternoon in northeastern PA
a ring of sparrows at this window   how many

days left   will they come to teach us?

                                      JUNE 10, 2020

Book XXII

There is this   clarity   when morning
arrives   not astonished

            after dreams to write
       phrases of acknowledgement—'daughter on a street vigil
                   returning without fear'

And the sentence   forms itself
in morning light   absence like a palm

covering the right side of one's face

in medias res.

◆

These sentences from H.D.'s
Paint It Today
coming into the mix
this morning—

      'There are so many different ways of thinking you
      see things. You can imagine. That is one process.
      You can go to sleep and dream an ordinary dream.
      That is another way.'

The proposition   to dream inside of thought
move among the word roads

           enchanted or barely capable
      route of prophecy or road of instruction

To return as the poem does
to dreams   segmented realities

changeable as weather   deepening
reddening inside the lens

       'finding the next ford in the river'

◆

    Out walking   you say it's dark some
where   it's a hinge inside your left arm
        twisting back the crease

    layer by layer   what's privileged here
what's pure absence   speaking out
        against the odds?

Sumac   elm   English rose   rhodoendron

The world of one's sight   proposing
an economy   built on such few

objects

    apparent in a row.

◆

'When we touch it we are safe.'

Recognition's oblique   incognito
appearance
    Noon bells of Our Lady of Mt. Carmel   the slowly

         turning wave of light
                              passing like a bridge across us.

  ◆

We are less   salient
brought up to hear   aggression

in the counter-sign   as an
appeal distinguished us

as weaker   in the eyes
of those who came before

Heroic simple   place
to be   in the world

shapely shepherded   orphan's
haunt

         raised on sweet braided grass.

◆

And was I faithless   turning
to receive such gifts   an economy

of hope   legated   spilled-over
these days of quarantine—

         Wind is making its progress
         across the lot   separate strands of
                  afternoon light

I'll visit them again later….

◆

It's not to celebrate chronology   but assert
its difficulty   'we were inside a stream
                of language—without defense'

So you could say   not so much inside
or outside   but a catachresis

of method & sensation   'Let the garden   aquatic
dream-like   overtaken by storms & weeds   form a circle

and let that circle   encircle   re-encircle   one by one   the properties
        of a self   so you can say   it was chance.'

◆

And what comes back   licensed
as 'ours'   You were right

to point out   'they are often really out of time (two to three
            years before an event the dream appears to depict) and/or
            I've seen things I haven't been able to get others to understand.'

Which is a form of kinship here   whatever one draws
from the past   recurrent as it is

                dormant histories   we're left rummaging through

            on our own.

◆

Sitting past the hour   I said I would
      come out of it   let the poem
   rest   awaiting the new day—

'The River reaches to my feet'

until I can't stand   in one place
but let my eyes rove

           the heavens   starless at midday

              noontides along the Delaware   come home
                      to proclaim their passage....

◆

As it stands   in print
1863   she wrote

      'Not "Revelation" - 'tis - that waits,
      But our unfurnished eyes - '

Kept inside   these years of
waiting
      formal   notational   spacers on level ground

When reading I saw it first as   'unfinished'

A kind of blurring   where the word
separates   mind & sight
         coupling   doubled

Like this hour   I'm moving outside
while my hands are still here   on keys

              'locked to fit daylight'

                                        JUNE 11, 2020

Book XXIII

Book XXIII

Where renewal is   this prayer woken
from a reading of Isaiah—

    'Let me sing for my beloved
      my love song concerning his
        vineyard'

When the world is broken   singing in this
site   through locality's loss   bride shepherd song

Not song but rite   not rite but aperture

Material writing   as location seeps
into discrepant arc
        I arranged the books in a
        stack—

        everything to be taken
        from words.

◆

Norma Cole, "From the Threshing Floor":

There was no way that they could find any crime
that I'd done, except where I was born, my origin
   —Habsiyyat, Prison Songs, trans. Paul Smith

A form of pity   from the scattered
body   a sign of antipathy
      we're acknowledging what is here—

Rites of passage   the angelic
voice   is burned through   as if

        stillness   a burning in the sky
     regions of stillness
               after strong rains—

Sometimes the body is in place   steady

common to itself   hands that take up

the vines of a grapevine   we are reading

of the shepherd's work   to follow through

      his read / unread

      beginnings…

◆

Passing through   over
segments of the passing tale
where 'was' is someplace else
to begin again

Word fever   my mother
drew a map on plain paper
of where we were—

     'Lift your head up, see what it looks like,'

     to permit some seeing through   lifelong

     looking the other direction

◆

Exile: "Esse est percipi," wrote Bishop Berkeley, being is being seen, being known. Ovid (43 BCE – 17/18 CE) wrote the *Tristia* from beyond the horizon of his known world, far from his language context, far from his companions, his witnesses, in mere space he could not recognize and value as place (found in Norma Cole).

I'm turning   where water is going to become
a sign   the language is restorative   we say
it's a sign from afar   the very earth
you live on   a sign

of having been here   moved across
from one land to another

       partition's eagle   slowmoving
           across the eastern frontier
     we're bending so far back
             south moving Greek

       alleged to have lived here once.

◆

And somehow to walk through   the way light
is waking us   patches of dawn   skips
    a beat   we're looser in the dawn
  era   to come back from sleep
           death's knot—

Slippage of the body   let it re-surface   become

a bearer   a boat of many tidings

Angel of passage

♦

Vallejo rests at the side
of what we're after—

   Va corriendo, andando, huyendo
  de sus pies...

The intricacy of movement   of a body in
flight   he is running, walking fleeing

from himself   the meaning of it
plain enough   to enter paradise   rice

thrown on the square   hearing is pure
stance   when you come upon him

running with clouds   the orphan
mingling with no one

   de tanto huir

Believer   stretch our your legs   run
with him across the plains

of dispossession   Argentina...

◆

Infinite sky writing....

◆

      'There is no silence
except in the mind'
              says Paz—

I'm driven back   to starters
with Thoreau in hand again
from his *Journals*—

'As we float down the river through
the still & hazy air–enjoying the
June-like warmth–see the first
kingbirds on the bare black willows //
with their broad white breasts & white
tipped tails–and the sound of the
first bobolink was floated to us //
from over the meadows–
                    May 13, 1855

Not river we saw   but sat there   at the side
of it   located by sound   objects
to refine the senses   word maps

      '& white
tipped tails'

        We can summon the dead   for everything
written is a death   speaking back
                        to the living.

♦

Which is lament
sequenced with   impoverishment
    to splay our body
  fresh in summer air—

        chords of light
     strands of cowrie shells
           bent over wire.

♦

Dear empty
skin   sky
    light—

I'm drawing
a blank
    on your pages.

Lifted from
another's
   hand.

♦

To experience Thursday then Friday
light is moving across the room
where my wife is standing   inside
the light is another woman beside
her my eyes were working back-
ward to see them to hold the two
in one—

    It's the fringe
of self selves
      turned back

  on themselves.

                June 12, 2020

Book XXIV

> *For a month past life has been a thing incredible to me. None but the kind gods can make me sane- If only they will let their south winds blow on me. I ask to be melted.*
>
> Thoreau, April 11, 1852

Not invention   but in situ
the wiring coming loose   in my hands

the fabric has become frayed   Older
days stretch back   undone

seamless   correspondences

     There is this evocation
   of time   a principled reaction
        to movement

     eventuality's highwire act
we are chastened by
        causation & incident

◆

*What is it drove us to these
locations not others?*

The casualness of reception   borders
we cross   step from inside of

a boundaried place   Ohio or Maryland
Athens is situated where the sky

goes thick   we can see mountain
& sea   from one window   inheritance

of this band of water   primitive
out of time

        this anticipatory wheel   reckoning
            far from native ground.

◆

And god talk
stops where the river
goes silent.

Near enough to land
a region we're seeing less & less of.....

◆

This morning thirst......

Another sign
of dislocation.

'I remember I remember'

Sovereign drawings
left out in the sun, their lines
of crayon

merging.

◆

And somehow it's common
enough   dreaming is part of prospect's

region   we come inside awhile   the lake
recedes   where water was the color

of sky   pitched high   we can swim
underneath   a warren of daytime stars

so heavy the body   dreams it is
a merchant   passing across these lanes

of river   did one ever invent the self
to realize its desolation?

◆

    If you run up
against the sides of it
       what will you see?

    Calm waters
Chesapeake stillness that is
       stillness akin.

◆

Wieners—

    'The story is not done.
    There is one wall
      left to walk. Yeah—'
Drifting in the company
of men   lone accompanist

of these poems   our melancholy
angels   directing us to other

days.

◆

It is a version of real time   spliced together
the poems are serial objectives   run into the light
you can stand
                    apart from a window   apparatus of the frame

You can become   one space inside
another   now this one returns   spectacular
what the heart can hold
                              apposite fiction   feral child's

Octave   let go of its body
become a thing of the world.

◆

Encampment   one could say 'you live here to say *here*'

Or did we mean to write   'entrapment'

when the spirit flees the body   enclosure's long

mouth   darkened   supple lips

heavenly attunement   /   atonement

          'The sunrise scatters'   a refinement

of decision   mind's tactful negligence

when the hand is so kind   to transfer
us across...

◆

It is a Tuesday in June   the light is
cloud-pocked   from outside   a grey sparrow

held in its movements   another follows to rest
on the steel plant hanger   indefinite time

closes over us   like hidden vertices
spanning the days   'What can you hide

inside your shelter, what can you
produce there?'

Lately I'm seeing the blue boats pass   from one side
to the other   And the spheres of light

                dominion's casuistry...

◆

'If we could be attentive to the same degree
in the presence of a human being.' (Weil)

◆

'Confused….a past reading'

that we invent the particulars of trees & other objects
in the world   give them names

from an index of eternity.

◆

We are late   you are saying
to come back to these few things—

The ground you saw yesterday   drenched
by rainstorms overnight   now is another

element of the world   here & again
plurality is a sign of effort   to keep oneself

here on solid ground   where the day is
not special nor unusual   but ongoing

rhythmic as light   storms across the horizon
somatic in their effect

              transient states   balk at stopping.

◆

'Such an afternoon.
Such wind.'

And rivers that are renewed
by signs

pressed onto parchment.

      As the alder floats
      upon the flood.

◆

It's here we say   'Father I'm one
you are two'

And become the witness   unfolding   shaped
by light across a bridge in June   not names

but their aftermath   'threading mazes
of unwearied thought'   we are accompanists

drowned at the river's edge

          to hold fancy   sweetened

          by these traces

                    'Everyone of its order, but will run on'

◆

When I'm taking   faith
for words   in place
of Love—

Here is summary
of affects

near and dear   we leave
these things
at the water's edge…

♦

Pirated   unplotted   simply to
negotiate the rhythmic
                   traces—

Daylight follows night work
in scenes borrowed
        from childhood   reading

through the nights   radio's dim
clock light under the cover
of darkness.

Thinking of how it comes
so late in life   no one's saying anything
otherwise—

But it's a kind of movement   necessary
to find   to keep
        song & singer alive.

Left for a spell   what habitat
can we make   brought back memories

        Until later we're not sure
how we came to drift
             apart from them.

◆

Walking side by side   my boy's arm looped
in another's   passing across the mall

at sundown   we sat by the river
to watch the men with their poles   near sundown

fishing   no escaping we weren't
company   but kept watch   leaning into

each catch   as we'd been taught
somehow   to move as others do

in the world.

JUNE 15, 2020

Book XXV

What could have been
   coda   or merely code
for existence
         that left me speechless—

      'All suffering
      which does not detach us
      is wasted suffering.'

Read in the morning
light   to coexist with Weil's
   emphatic detachment
      from the world of
    material things

as we are making   what is
nameless here   a book of signs
   codex for skin's
         deposit.

◆

 And rain later   or warm
to see the sun   you said it was
robins at nightfall
        heard again through
     the screened door—

willingness to become the calls   inimitable
        birds   I can't see or properly name.

◆

The house—
not seen in 60
years

       in the course of things we
   recall the necessary objects
           refined by memory

They teach us to observe
against our willingness
                  these addresses to place.

◆

'To lose someone: we suffer because the
departed, the absent, has become something
imaginary and unreal. But our desire for him
is not imaginary. We have to go down into
ourselves to the abode of the desire which is
not imaginary. Hunger: we imagine kinds of
food, but the hunger itself is real: we have to
fasten on the hunger. The presence of the
dead person is imaginary, but his absence is
very real: henceforward it is his way of appearing.'

       And sought there   what was it?

       Framing language for a study   of disintegration

       not of the social   quietly the material

　　　　　is distinct　separate from us　we move

　　　　　among the dead　　as light does

　　　　　imaged there　intact　a way of re-appearing.

◆

We're inside
or the day is
out there—

habits resume
work

all day the motors
of the mowers
run across grass

I have time
to spare　black
soil cut into

squares.

◆

As Olson in *Maximus Book Three* puts
this image in mind—

　　　　　　'The river runs now
　　　　　　as free & clear as drinking
　　　　　　water--& on the bench
　　　　　　opposite the bridge tender

    the second time up the bridge
     goes and through it from
    the harbor comes
    the same
    Trina Lea
     Newbury port
   old &
    gillnetter
   [came through the moon was
       so swollen]'

We have tread carefully
across   to meet him
in the middle   of late life.

Stains on our shirt   we're laying
things down   wearing what we

have   day after day.

◆

What's common   held
here   in common   this
instruct to re-read

Olson's language in light of this
from *Rivers of the Anthropocene*—

  'Earlier in the geological epoch
the sea rose and retreated from the islands
of what would become Southeast Asia.
Rain-fed rivers drained the valleys
with marine sediment.   Thousands

of years later, in colonial times, a
main thoroughfare was established
on top of the marine sediment of
one such ancient seabed.'

◆

Whence Orchard Road   where a sea
was   sediment from the valley

becomes the new world   of seeing
where we are   in these fissures

of historic time

       where night soil was collected
            and brought to the farms
                     uphill.

◆

There is no reason
to stay here   or elsewhere
    among these artifacts

of human consciousness.

I want to understand
one place long enough   to withstand
delusion   realism's

after image.

◆

    'I'm running my hands
over nude grass   the light when
      I find you—

     draws you near.'

As though despair   were an ideogram
written into our flesh   one picture

of detached becoming   asserting itself.

◆

'We met you on the path   late in the day
you said it was the same path   you traveled
90 years ago as a girl in London—

    I held out my hand in greeting
      as you passed
                  on the path.'

When yesterday   you came downstairs
dressed in blue cotton   said it's time
to have some sun   as I watered the garden
tending to roses
         spotted with rust.

◆

  'This town lies out under the sky—a port of entry
and departure for souls to and from Heaven.'

A willingness to recognize
the passage of ourselves
through each other

we are gifted by what we
don't enact or trace
to ourselves

the immediacy of
presences we can't
verify or deny.

Here is clothing for the journey....

◆

Listening
at the door—

      'in separation the red bloom opens'

One is moving away
from oneself   we say
he is chastened

by what he sees

Black letters
of our dead   'the waves

of morning'

Blue of the bluer tongue.

JUNE 16, 2020

Book XXVI

Woke to a waning
crescent   near 4 a.m.

sat on edge of our bed   keeping
steady by the walls   movement

is less assured   so early
our body in fits & starts

steadying itself...

        forward time   full moon
  four days ahead   2:41 a.m.
           low tide just before
              at 2:34 a.m.

    Delaware's long coast   blackened under stars.

◆

We are living parallel
lives—
      to say this as root
form of knowledge

         There is the world
outside any of us   another attached
              to formation—

So to journey here   is to situate
self apart from others   to learn
the way independent
         of the social   precarity's

elongated gait   hovering at the
water's edge   low tide
                    alert as light

is across the shoreline   low scene
of movement   stasis   bending

to receive instruction.

◆

Everything can be water & light   nothing
      can say what will endure
   after water & light
             are gone.   Dreamt

I was dipped in oil of the castor plant
        kiki along the riverbanks
   sown into their soil
              my arms dipped

in kiki oil so that I resumed
        travel among my people
     estranged familiar presence
             tracing my people's journey

to restore lamp light   oil of the
     kiki plant   restoring them.

◆

       When every day   rites
are simple to reproduce
            gather the plants

    lay them inside the
garden bed moist lines of grass
      folded among rose blooms

    & hydrangea leaves—

To return where my garden is a rite
of simple action taken in world
time

    Out of need to tend
    re-store
      our human part.

◆

    Or the orders
are permission re-written as light
    on the backs of book jackets

      I've delayed how many
years? awaiting what form
    of recovery dented light

      stops at the open door
where our ancestors
        rise again to meet us—

    'Not knowing when the dawn
will come' return makes its angle
        clearest here folded

wings of the mourning dove
  clear light when she rises
    fed by movement
          apart from our own

◆

      And privacy   some semblance
of the real   among these traces
       of person/s   opaque quiescent pursuit

bluer along the track

           'curtained....behind a darkened moon.'

◆

If all
we have
are these—

    'West of my lodge   mulberries
  leaves ready for picking   by the
             riverbank   irises

     fragrant   sweet as honey'

◆

Low rinsed light
sour taste of tannin
     back of our throat.

A month and another month…

Our public song.

JUNE 17, 2020

Book XXVII

Book XXVII

Rains as they come   during
a long storm   she goes outside
stands under skies
                    opening   the rain

pouring down—

Not trees but their disappearance   noted
in the foreground   a block of cedars
taken down last season   No way
to reassert their presence

                 Light storms   from inside
a small part of the landscape
                        these renewals of the body

sufficient   enabled by will.

◆

The history of oneself   of little
importance   to others   what can
we say   *We're here*   as any
one else might be

'Not of this world' you said
by which you meant
                    'Not here'

◆

Reading Enslin   to find
the voice   he was asserting
capable of signs   single put
a man of his word—

Not staggered by death   but at the
forefront of saying   'I am here now'
Stooped these years later
to pick up the book
               off the staircase   put it
       back down   weighted
                     glass in one hand—

He was talking over
my head.

◆

Memory is lapidary   crisscrosses
mental life   separated from its
sources—
       torqued here & there
   by what reunites us
            sensation's purview

      steady on our feet
  to earn the days
         afterward

      warm moon light
   indigo call
        town's abeyant

                  sanctity.

◆

To open out   one world
in place of another

'Safe keeping'   some language
forgot us   another part

kept us here—

      Inscriptions at the side of the road
    we left our directions in the car
         headed east into Ohio...

◆

'Bird feathers, flowers'
Keido wrote in 1787

He died on the seventh
day of the fourth
month

Age 73

◆

    'The river runs now
    as free and clear as drinking
    water—'

Cloth thrown onto a bed at sundown.
No one lives apart from their belongings.

I'm cleaning the kitchen floor   waiting for your
return   Ghostly figuration

Daughter   Mother

        A sign sent ahead to find us.

◆

        Ragged anemone   sent
out for it   to name it again
                when seen—

      light cast shelter   on numerous
carpels   forming an oblong to
             subcylindric head.

So we sit with our book of
                wildflowers

located inside a fold of late afternoon
light
        and voice is lower now

serrated by shadows   industrious
querulous body of shapes & designs

We live to answer their call.

◆

To image the wild calla   as if
it were profit borne of
             human labor—

'perennial herb of swamps
& bogs   with long acrid root
................stocks

covered with sheathing
scales   and fibrous roots
at the nodes   from which rise
................numerous petioled leaves

with thick entire glossy green
broadly ovate or suborbicular leaf
blades
........2 to 5 inches wide   cuspidate or pointed
........at the apex   and deeply cordate at the base.'

Writing it out   in black ink
to keep the image intact.

◆

That I could give such things
to you
........forward of your lived affect—

Eventually to find you   in the aftermath
of reading   silent companion
inside each story   I could re-tell
you.

................So little comes through   where & when & how
............you are not even 'you'   though a surface
........................of elegant words surrenders your voice

................back to me...

◆

In truth   returning
the way we came

street by street   storm clouds
passing   eastern quadrant

of sky   sunlit

Hard to distill   life
movements   mnemonic

half-steps into the dark
flowers   we can't yet name

or identify on sight.

◆

As children we sat   spellbound
by the arrangement
................of letters on a plain background

And drew them over and over
patterns of letters
................on a grey background

Syllabics of habitual counting

$$5 + 5 + 7 \;/\; 7 \;/\; 7$$

◆

As article of faith
to comb the books   for safety
or an arrangement
of words   that will cohere—

pillaging her lines
 blackened skies
orchard setting

      'Night
          the sag
             of day'

Tablecloth put inside the closet
with blankets & towels.

Her version of arithmetic
to stand still
        at the river's edge   her pockets full
                            of stones.

◆

A quiet flock
of geese   notations
on a grey background

Skin & Sight   Unseen.

♦

       The woman I'm recalling
  gave birth to another
            child—

Spoke to him in Greek   said his name
without influence.

       Impossible to recall—
 stagnant waters
           where her days came to

    an end   black square of Athenian
            light—

  Laid to rest there   birds in the rafters
     of her village lair.

♦

[Dream]

    I woke with my hands
  at my sides   & arms
        of a woman

    embraced me   laid me
down in the orchard   near Hadley MA
      so that I couldn't move

    outside the circle   of her
embrace   but saw in her eyes
      our finitude as beings set

    down here forever….to pass through our days
emptied of desire or need   without bread or water
      casuists to the end.

                                            DOYLESTOWN, PA
                                            28 SEPTEMBER 2019-18 JUNE 2020

NOTES

The epigraph is from *George Oppen: Selected Prose, Daybooks and Papers*, edited with an introduction by Stephen Cope. Connections drawn in Oppen's "Daybooks" between politics, writing and poesis played a significant role in the thinking-through of questions raised by some of the poems included here. These Daybooks were written under the signs of many writers, living and dead, represented below.

BOOK I: Ezra Pound, *Canto LVI*: 'dark fur from a hare's ear,' 'And under the almond trees gods with them.'

BOOK II: Du Fu: 'the Pleiades almost / nameless….the moon tilted /and halfgone.'

BOOK III. Roy Fisher: 'my agenda consists in not having one.' and 'The "I" is my unexamined label.' John Clare: 'Meet me by the sweetbriar, / By the mole-hill swelling there.'

BOOK IV: Rachel Blau DuPlessis: 'We live in nomadic unfulfillment.' Robert Duncan: 'Waves are not the same as deepwater.' Natalie Diaz: 'this is my American labyrinth'. Richard Burton, *Anatomy of Melancholy*: 'the air works in all men.'

BOOK V: Vallejo: 'Let's not go in, it frightens me…' Whitman: 'the glory of the stars…'

BOOK VI: Jabès, 'Faces for Antonio Saura': 'Turn, toward me, your face.' Ed Roberson: 'the place where crying begins.' Hölderlin: 'Each of us reaches for the place.'

BOOK X: Henry David Thoreau, *Journals,* February 9, 1854: 'There is a peculiar softness and luminousness in the air this morning.'. Virgil, *Georgics:* 'The Sun will give Signs.' Layli Long Soldier 'whereas / I rose and placed my eyes and tongue on a shelf.' Rachel Blau DuPlessis: 'not here to decorate my age,' in an interview with DuPlessis conducted by the author.

BOOK XII: Elizabeth Gray, *Salient:* 'So it is said / that instead of wooden crosses they have names / planted in space.'

BOOK XV: H.D.'s *Helen in Egypt* is the source of the language beginning, 'There was always another.'

BOOK XVI: Robert Duncan, from 'Often I Am Permitted to Return to a Meadow': 'east against the source of the sun.'

BOOK XVII: Whitman: 'With departing Venus, large to the last, Agamben, *The Coming Community*: 'We have only hope.' Robert Duncan, from *The H.D. Book*: 'What returned to my thought as I began work this morning.' Oppen: 'All this is obvious,'

BOOK XIX: Simone Weil: 'Pythagorean idea: the good is always defined.' Witold Gombrowiscz, *The Diaries*: 'in an even more bottomless night.'

Book XX: W.C. Williams, *Paterson*, 'It was lighted in those days by candles.' The circus scene depicted in this passage refers to the Barnum & Bailey route from 1891 that took the circus through Paterson on May 5, 1891. Du Fu: 'Clear autumn in the / Wu Gorges, ten / thousand ravines lament'

Book XXV: Simone Weil: 'All suffering which does not detach us is wasted suffering.' Jason M. Kelly, Rivers of the Anthropocene: 'Earlier in the geological epoch….' Whitman: 'I'm running my hands / over nude grass.' Thoreau: 'This town lies out under the sky—a port of entry and departure for souls to and from Heaven.'

www.ingramcontent.com/pod-product-compliance
Lightning Source LLC
Chambersburg PA
CBHW011406070526
44577CB00003B/386